Best Kept

Canadian Immigrant

Secrets

ANDREA VILLANUEVA - CHIU

ISBN: 9798728913368

This is for you, soon-to-be immigrant to Canada.

CONTENTS

Introduction

Migrating is difficult.

It becomes even more difficult if you don't have family or friends who can help you along the way.

Although you can research and read about Canada before you arrive, nothing beats first-hand experience and lessons from people who have actually gone through it.

Done it and succeeded.

I migrated to British Columbia, Canada in 2015, along with my husband and two children.

Just like you, my husband and I were worried about the new life we would have in Canada.

I lay awake at night wondering what life really was in store for us in Canada. We were unsure if we were making the right decision.

How do you get a job before your savings run out?

Do you really need to juggle two to three jobs just to make ends meet?

How do you adjust to a diverse culture?

Where can you find new friends?

I looked for resources that could hopefully provide me with more information.

I wanted to know what Canadian immigrant life looked like, but all I heard were sad, horrifying stories of why we shouldn't pursue migration.

Although there are plenty of helpful organizations in Canada, their focus is mainly on job hunting. You can access them only when you already have a valid visa to Canada.

Fortunately, we were able to get a job in less than 60 days.

What's even better?! We were paid well above the minimum wage!

In less than six months, we were able to provide our kids with a Canadian education savings program that will help them pay for their education.

In less than two years, we were able to buy our own home.

More than luck, our mindset coupled with our actions made this happen, and I am happy to share this with you all.

Over the past six years, I have gathered lessons and experiences that could make living and settling in Canada easier.

A lot of these I wish I had known before we landed in Canada.

Most were not taught at the Canadian orientation we attended.

We had to figure out most of it on our own.

You might think that getting a job is just about sending resumes to as many companies as you can.

Or you can just Google about how to save and grow your money every month.

Or you can just ask Canadian friends and families about how to get back the taxes you paid to the CRA.

But you don't have to do this alone.

You don't have to do this by trial and error.

You don't have to make the same mistakes we did.

Join me on this journey to learn the secrets on how to make Canadian employers hire you.

Read through this book to learn about the Canadian way of life in order to minimize culture shock.

You'll also be able to manage your expectations by learning about the facts versus the myths about living in Canada.

This book is not exclusively aimed at immigrants already in Canada.

This book will also serve those who are seriously considering migrating to Canada.

This book will give you a glimpse of life as a Canadian immigrant.

This book will help you decide if you will continue with your Canadian immigration plans.

Sit back, relax and let me guide you on how to adjust to your new life in Canada.

Let me share my experiences.

I want you to know that you too can be successful in Canada - even if it means making a few sacrifices.

Are you ready? Let's get started!

What Does Success Look Like To You?

"Success is the continual unfolding of the design of your own life and pulling it off. That's what success is." -Jim Rohn-

In 2013, I was a newly promoted manager at the biggest telecom company in the Philippines.

I am happily married with two kids.

We lived in a 3-bedroom townhouse, owned a car and had 2 helpers.

I just turned 30 years old.

You'd say I was already successful at that.

But that same year, I resigned from my high paying and prestigious job. Decided to be a housewife instead while keeping myself open to online job opportunities.

Shortly after that, my family moved to Dubai for my husband's work assignment.

A year later, we migrated to Canada. We started all over again.

We had to leave our jobs and work in entry level positions in industries we didn't even have experience in.

We've had to rebuild our savings depleted by immigration.

Fast forward to 2021.

I am a freelancer for two businesses.

My family now has four kids.

We live in a 2-bedroom condo; no helpers, no cars.

Guess when I felt more successful?

Now.
Today.
The present.

Back in 2013, I was living my life based on what our culture expected me to do, so as not to disappoint other people, to keep up with my peers, and to make "use" of my education.

When all I really wanted was to be home with my kids instead of having to be at my desk 9am-5pm (at least).

When all I really wanted was to cook meals for my family, instead of having a helper cook for us.

When all I really wanted was to pick up my kids from school, walk to the nearby store and have snacks with them. Instead of having a school bus pick them up.

Today, I may be living in a smaller house without the conveniences of a car or a helper, but I've never felt more free.

Free from rushing from one schedule to the next.
Free from thinking about what other people might say.

Free to live my life as I wanted to (without being irresponsible, of course).

I am still in the process of "charting my own course."

Yet, even when designing my life today, I still have to "weigh the costs."

"It's not the money. It's not the success. You've got to make sure everything works. Not something at the expense of everything." - Jim Rohn

At the end of each day, I must remember why I chose this life.
Why we chose to be in Canada.
Why we decided to leave our comfortable lives behind

It's my family.

Canadian Dream Busters:
Myths that will make your Canadian dream a nightmare

"Replaying the past over and over again will only ruin your present. Let it go. A brand new future awaits." -Robert Tew-

Three highly paid professionals from different countries arrive in Canada as permanent residents.

Andy is a top-notch doctor from Singapore.
Knowing that there's a shortage of doctors in Canada, he applied for physician jobs right away.

Beth is a teacher at one of the international schools in the Middle East. She wanted to learn more about the Canadian education system so she applied for babysitting jobs in the meantime.

Carrie is a highly-paid accountant at a multinational company in the Philippines. She wanted to get a job as soon as possible so she applied for any job she saw.

A fast food clerk?
A supermarket cashier?
Or even as a cleaning lady?

It didn't really matter!

As long as Carrie felt she was qualified, she would apply.

Two months into the job search, Andy and Beth are both frustrated with their job prospects.

Their money's running out.
No one's even calling them for an interview!

Meanwhile, Carrie is now happily employed at a supermarket chain.
She sleeps well at night without worrying about money.

A lot of new immigrants have what I call the Canadian Dream Busters.

These are myths that will make your Canadian dream a nightmare if not controlled right away.

They can lead to a disappointing, miserable immigrant life.

It stops you from enjoying the good life that Canada has to offer.

Canadian Dream Buster #1:
"My job is in demand in Canada.
Getting a job will be easy."

On our first week in our newly rented apartment, we were excited to go shopping.

We wanted to buy furniture to put in our new house.

By the time we arrived at the bus stop, Anna was already there.

After a few pleasantries and some stories, we learned that Anna was from the same country as us.

Upon learning this, she greeted us and welcomed us to Canada with sarcasm, even saying: "Oh, welcome to Canada, where dreams come true!"

We were in shock.

We would have left right then and there, if not for the bus arriving sooner!

She was so unhappy and bitter you wouldn't want to hang around with her.

Apparently she was a teacher back home who now works as a cleaning lady in Canada. She's been cleaning houses for a long time and she already sees herself retiring as a cleaner.

For her, Canada wasn't what she hoped for.

In her mind, she had just wasted her life moving to Canada.

Many new immigrants expect to be able to work in the same industry right away.

Even worse, they expect to earn the same income they used to earn back home.

Sadly, this is not the case.

Remember that Canada has its own culture and it has its own professional regulations you have to familiarize yourself with either through education or experience.

In the meantime, be proud of whatever job you're starting out with.

Whether that's in the grocery store, as a fast food worker or even as a cleaner.

Remember, that's just the start.

No one, nothing, is stopping you from being what you want to be.

You just have to keep working on yourself, learning new skills or going back to school if that's what's needed.

Canadian Dream Buster #2:
***"I don't need to go back to school -- I have a good
education, lots of credentials and work experience."***

Can I ask you a question?

How soon do you think you'll be able to go back to the work you used to do?

Do you think six months is enough?
A year, maybe.
Or in three years?

Will it take you five years?

More than 20% of Canadian jobs are regulated for the safety and well-being of
Canadians.

When we first arrived in Canada, my husband was okay with being a janitor.

He thought it was easy to get a janitorial job because back home, anyone can
be a janitor as long as you know how to clean the house.

He applied for any janitorial post he saw.

After a lot of interviews, he wasn't accepted to any janitorial post because
apparently you have to have a building services worker certification for most
janitorial jobs.

A building service worker program is like a six to eight week course where they teach you the proper cleaning and proper sanitation of buildings and facilities.

It gives you a higher chance of landing a janitorial job.

I also have a friend named Rosa who is a chef, teacher, and bakeshop owner.

Obviously, it was easy for her to get accepted to Tim Hortons or to Wendy's for a job.

However, she was still required to get a food safety certificate before she was able to start working.

In Canada, it is important to always upgrade and up-skill yourself if you want to work in the same industry that you used to work in.

In some cases, you even need to get a license or a certificate to be allowed to work in that industry.

Would you like to know your occupation is regulated in Canada?
Check it out at this link: bit.ly/RegulatedOccupation

If later on you realize that you don't want to go back to your industry.

Or it will take you a very long time to go back, read on to the next Dream Buster...

Canadian Dream Buster #3:
"I wasted all my years of schooling and work experience. I'm doing a totally unrelated job. I'm not even earning close to what I used to earn back home."

I have good news for you!

Your education?
Your work experience?

They're not wasted at all!

I'm serious, I'm not kidding!

When you were accepted as an immigrant to Canada, your work experience came with a lot of transferable skills.

Those skills are the ones you can use for any job you decide to pursue in Canada.

You see, there are two types of skills:

One is the hard skills or the technical skills.
These are mandatory job requirements.
They can only be learned through diploma or specialized training.

Examples include performing surgery, developing a lesson plan, making a financial statement or even operating equipment like a forklift.

The second type is called soft skills.

These are skills that can easily be used in more than one work environment and gained through experience.

And these are transferable skills.
Other examples of transferable skills include writing reports, dealing with clients, working for a team or even answering the phone.

On my first week of job hunting, I was approached by an insurance agent for training.

My background in accounting and my skills in budgeting, financial analysis and an eye for detail make me a perfect fit to be an insurance agent.

I know a lot of accountants who stayed with this line of work, eventually setting up their own businesses and forming their own teams.

I also have a lot of friends who were chefs from different countries who initially worked as restaurant servers.

Their skills in food handling, customer service, and ability to work in a stressful environment, make them the perfect fit to work in the food industry.

According to Nick Noorani's Nine Soft Skills No Immigrants Should Be Without, most immigrants arrive with 90% technical skills and only 10% soft skills.

But what employers are looking for is 60% soft skills.
From here, you can already see the misalignment.

	What Immigrants Have	What Employers Want
Soft Skills	10%	60%
Technical Skills	90%	40%

The tendency for new immigrants is to go back to school.
But this only increases the hard skills and not necessarily the soft skills.

As they say:
"Hard skills will get you an interview, but you need soft skills to get and be able to keep the job".

Soft skills are often cultural.

Here is an example:
Small talk is not common in our country.

When a stranger approaches you and starts small talk, it's a sign to run in the opposite direction.

But in Canada, small talk is common.

Not acknowledging it even with a simple greeting or even with a smile is considered rude.

Soft skills will determine whether you are the right fit for the company.
It will also determine if you're able to connect with your coworkers and your office mates.

Canadians are known to be "painfully polite."

"Painfully polite" means they say "sorry" for almost anything.
Yes, even if it's not their fault.

There are actually a lot of memes and a lot of jokes online about Canadians having to say sorry at least 10 times in order to maintain their citizenship.

I once had a coworker named Kate who was often absent.
She'll be absent at least once or even twice a week.

If she hasn't clocked in by 7:00 AM, you can be sure that she's already absent for the entire day.

That left us, her coworkers, covering most of her work.

The next day, when she comes back, you won't even hear a "thank you" or a "sorry" for being absent.
That made her unpopular among her Canadian colleagues.

Eventually, Kate left the company because she was unable to make friends with anyone else.

Can I ask you more questions?

What about you?
Are you willing to adapt to this new culture or would you rather stick to what you grew up with?

Remember, your answer will determine your success in the Canadian job market.

To make this hard skills and soft skills lesson stick with you, I created a puzzle that lists the nine soft skills.

Unscramble the letters to come up with soft skills that you can later put in your Canadian-style resume. At the bottom of the puzzle is a hidden message that says what you should do with these soft skills.

Check you answers at: http://bit.ly/sofskillsanswerkey

Soft Skills Every Immigrant Should Have

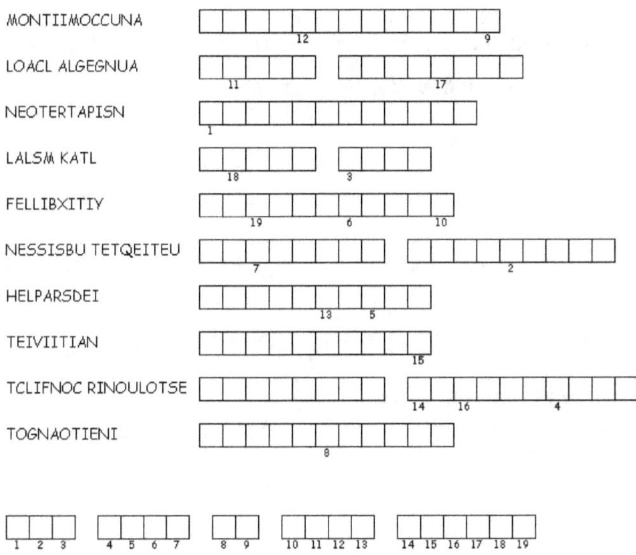

Unscramble each of the clue words.
Copy the letters in the numbered cells to other cells with the same number.

Source: Nick Noorani's Nine Soft Skills No Immigrants Should Be Without

Too Busy Earning A Living
To Spend Time With Family?

"No amount of money or success can take the place of time spent with your family." -Anonymous-

When we were new in Canada, we kept hearing about "hallway relationships."

We discovered this is when married couples just meet in the hallway of their home to exchange keys and reminders.

One had just come home from work, and the other was now leaving for work.

That's why it's called hallway relationships - only in the hallway do they get to see and talk to each other.

That's even sadder than long-distance relationships! Physically together but still apart?

Why?

These are my theories:

1. Stay-in nannies and house helpers are not the norm in Canada.

No one will look after the kids when both parents are working.

Relatives usually live far away.

Parents usually need to make shifting schedules available to ensure someone is at home looking after the children.

2. Daycare is expensive.

Instead of paying for daycare, they just sacrifice their time together (saying it's only temporary).

They would rather keep what they are earning instead of allotting a portion of their income to daycare.

Most of the immigrants were foreign workers or expats. They're used to spending a lot of time away from their families to work.

While I understand all of this, that doesn't mean it should go on.

By now, it should be obvious how much I value family togetherness.

When we arrived in Canada, one of my non-negotiables was that nobody works the graveyard shift! Even if that means having to pay for daycare for two kids!

We migrated to Canada for a better quality of life - more family time, less stress, more happiness!

Yet we won't be together? Why did we move in the first place then?
We should have stayed in our country!

Most people would say, "But there's no other job!"
I personally don't believe this.

From my experience, there are lots of employment opportunities in Canada if you aren't picky in the beginning.

The O.N.E Secret to Make Employers Hire You

"It does not matter how slowly you go, as long as you do not stop."
-Confucius-

Now that you have complied with all the required paperwork to complete your immigration status...

Social insurance numbers, Health Cards, Permanent Resident Cards

Your next priority is to find a job!

You need to pay for that newly rented apartment that you will live in for the next months or even years!

You need to pay for the phone plan and wifi you signed up for.

You have to pay for your daily groceries.

In this section, we will discuss the O.N.E Secret to make employers hire you.

In this section, you will learn how to be irresistible to Canadian employers and stand out from other applicants.

Along the way you will be learning more about the free resources that are available and should be taken advantage of as a new immigrant.

They Were Hesitant to Hire me.
But When They Saw My Skills...

Let me tell you about my husband

My husband absolutely loves nature!

He loves nature so much that it was a deciding factor for him to choose British Columbia as our final destination in Canada.

He was so excited to go sightseeing when we arrived in BC!

And I would always be annoyed.

I wanted to tell him,
"Hello, we're not tourists here! We're not here to spend all the savings we brought from back home!"

You see between the two of us, I'm the more practical one.
My goal was to get a job as soon as possible.

His goal? To enjoy the sights and scenes of British Columbia.

I was so focused on getting a job so soon that instead of being bored at home and binging on library books, I decided to sign up for different training and seminars.

They're 100% free anyway!

Every day, I would bring my kids to daycare early so I could attend a seminar.

I would stay hours after the seminar ended to be able to use the computer.

I applied for various accounting jobs in Vancouver because it was the only job I knew how to do.

One day while walking around the neighborhood, I saw a job post.

A new Walmart store is about to open - five minutes from our house!

That same day I printed up my resume and submitted it to the hiring manager.

Fortunately, the hiring manager was a fellow Filipino.

She wanted to help me land my first job in Canada, but was hesitant because I had no Canadian experience.

Turns out, there are a lot of other Filipinos on the management team. So they looked at my soft skills.

One of them decided to hire me as one of her staff.

Within 60 days from our arrival, me and my husband were able to land a stable job.

They said that we were lucky to get a job so quickly because not many immigrants get to have a job that fast.

Which is why they require you to bring in at least six months worth of savings.

On average it takes six months for a new immigrant to find a job.
In my six years in Canada, I held two different jobs.

My husband held five different jobs in different industries and at different management levels.

It wasn't always easy to switch jobs.

Along the way, though, we learned different strategies and tricks to stand out.

To be called into that first interview!

And eventually become the one to be selected and hired for the position.

Introducing!

The O.N.E Secret to make employers hire you!

O.N.E is an acronym for Open. Network and Enroll.

Open Yourself to What Others Have Closed

I've always heard of the Canadian Experience, but only then did I realize how much it can make or break the selection process.

I'm sure you're asking,
But how can I have Canadian experience if I just arrived in Canada?

How can I have Canadian experience if companies don't want to hire me because I don't have Canadian experience?

It's like the proverbial chicken and egg question, eh?
Which came first, the chicken or the egg?

Secret number one: be open to any job at first.

While it is true that many companies seek Canadian experience, there are also companies that hire without Canadian experience.

In fact, these companies would be happy to hire newly landed immigrants in order to attract new workers.

The problem is that most immigrants don't enter these industries.

Why? Because this is where most immigrants have no experience of working.

Industries like groceries or retail, local stores, fast food companies, and even manpower agencies.

The only way to find out?

Be open to any job opportunities that come your way.

As long as you are willing to be trained, they'll be happy to hire you.

Do you remember Rosa from Section One?

She started off as a cashier and coffee server at Tim Hortons.
She is now a bookkeeper at a property management firm and a small business owner.

How about my husband who wanted to be a janitor first?
No, he wasn't a janitor right away.

He was offered a job at Walmart too, but turned down the offer.
He believed he was going to get a better paying job.

And here I am telling you not to be picky when it comes to jobs!

When he decided to turn down the offer, he went to a manpower agency and asked if they had any jobs for him.

The hiring manager asked: "What's your availability?"

He answered: "I'm open any day of the week, any time of the day. You can assign me to any shifts that you want."

That same day he was offered a warehouse job. He was required to report the next day.

That warehouse job proved to be a blessing to us and our family.

It allowed for regular salary increases and even trained him to operate an equipment which, later on, gave him a certification.
That opened the door for him to land a management position in retail.

Why look so far?

I was an accountant who became a supermarket lady.

I used to spend hours behind the computer analyzing numbers and solving problems to come up with management recommendations.

When I arrived in Canada, my job was to make sure that the shelves were fully stocked. Customers were assisted in making their purchases.

I have no regrets. I loved that job.
That remains to be the most fulfilling and most satisfying thing I've ever done.

I'd even say that was the least stressful of the jobs I held.
Most importantly, that was the Canadian experience I had.
It opened a lot of doors for me.

Eventually, I was able to transfer to an office job.
In the accounting department.

Yes! In downtown Vancouver!

No wonder I wasn't getting any calls no matter how many accounting jobs I applied for.

Most accounting jobs require Canadian experience.

Network Your Way To Job Opportunities

Secret number two: Network.
Network and connect, especially with people from your own country.

Do you know who helped me land that accounting job in downtown Vancouver?

Ask me: Who?

She is Lara, a friend from church.
Another Filipino!

I still remember the day I sent my application for that accounting job.
I was taking my lunch break at Walmart.

I was typing the cover letter on my phone, making sure to mention Lara's name on the cover letter to stand out from the other applicants.

In Canada, referrals are a big deal.

Companies would rather hire referrals instead of walk-ins.

The next day, I was surprised when I got called for an interview.

During the interview, the business owner asked, "Who is Lara?"

It turned out that Lara was not an employee.

Just a friend of an employee who happened to know about the job opening!

That definitely made for an icebreaker during the interview.

I'm sure that blooper made me stand out.
I was eventually hired for that position.

Just a word of warning, though.

Be sure to set your boundaries.
You still want to retain that privacy.

Examples of networking opportunities you can attend include networking events, meetup.com, Facebook groups, church and spiritual communities, and even neighbors and friends.

You can't imagine the gold mine that is in your network in relation to job opportunities.

Want To Be More Valuable For Free?

Secret number three: Enroll.
Enroll in almost any free immigrant resource you can.

These were the training sessions I attended when we first arrived:

New immigrant job search, which includes resume writing and an interview workshop; Soft skills training; and Mentoring.

The training did not happen all at the same time.

Usually, they would require you to attend basic training. That would then be the stepping stone or the foundation for the next training session.

Some training also requires qualifications and has certain criteria for you to be able to attend.

I remember working at Walmart, but I continued to attend mentoring sessions.

I know I eventually want to switch jobs.
I wanted to transfer to the industry I used to work.

Imagine braving a 45-minute trip by train and bus when I could have been home five minutes after my shift ended at Walmart.

The fall season was already over. It was starting to get cold and rainy.

Since this was the first cold season I'm about to experience, I started getting sick.

Nevertheless, I kept on attending because I didn't want to miss the opportunity of being mentored by someone already in the accounting field.

There are a lot of immigrant-serving organizations that you can look for by going to this link: http://bit.ly/helpforCanadiannewcomer

It doesn't list everything, however. I know there are a lot more that are not on this list. This is already a good start because it already lists several organizations in different provinces.

In British Columbia, these are the organizations that I personally transacted with or inquired with:

successbc.ca;
issbcbc.org;
mosaicbc.org; and
Welcomebc.ca

Quiz Time!

The question is:
How long should a resume be?

Five seconds to answer.

Five.
Four.
Three.
Two.
One!

How long should your resume be? What do you think?

Do you think it's three pages? Two pages?
Maybe one page?

The answer to that?

Just one page.

The Canadian-style resume only has one page.

This is why you need to learn to trim your resume.

Remove all irrelevant details.

Remove all work experiences that are irrelevant to the position you're applying for.

And yes! You read that right!

There's a Canadian style resume!

Would you like a one-on-one session to prepare a Canadian-style resume customized to your needs?

Would you like me to personally work with you to make your resume stand out from other applicants?

Send an email to familimigrant@gmail.com to apply.

Who Wants To Build Their Savings In 365 Days?
A new immigrant's guide to saving money each month

I was surprised when one of my friends, not just one, but several of my friends told me "You're not "in" when you don't have debts in Canada.

In Canada, credit cards are widely used.

Nearly all transactions are paid through credit cards.
Even small business owners accept credit card payments.

So it's easy to fall into the quicksand of debt.
I'm sure this is something you don't want to get stuck in.

Once you're there, it's a lot harder to get out of it.

In this section, you will learn about the lifestyle choices you can make to save money every month.

You will learn to save money faster and more automatically.

Every year, you will also learn how to leverage your expenses to get your money back.

Are you ready? Let's get started!

True or False?

Migrating is expensive.
What do you think?

This is very much true! Migrating is expensive.

When my family and I decided to move to Canada, we hired an immigration agency to help us with our immigration process.

That in itself is already twice if not even three times what we could have spent if we had just applied on our own.

Add to that the landing fee for a family of four.

IELTS for myself and my husband.

The minimum amount that should be in your bank account as required by immigration.

Oh, did I mention I was a full-time stay-at-home mom at the time?

I had no regular income, just a few part-time gigs.

When we received our visa, the spending didn't stop there.

We had to buy plane tickets for four people.

We had to book a three week stay at an Airbnb for the first few weeks after our arrival in Canada.

We had to pay for transportation costs to get around the city.
We had to pay for our long-term apartment deposit.

Expenses just kept coming!

It's as if money kept going out and nothing was coming back.
We didn't have jobs back then.

I know how you feel. I've been there.

I know how it feels to be spending for everything with nothing coming back.
Nothing's happening with your job hunt.

Fortunately, there are plenty of ways to save money.

While there's no escaping the expenses you need to incur to get to Canada, as well as the money you have to spend in your first few days of arrival, there are ways that you can save money -- and some of which you can get for free!

Introducing: A new immigrant's guide to making extra money each month!

Depending on your income and depending on the province you're located in, this might be different.

What I will be sharing is based on my experiences in British Columbia.

Turn Your Low Income Status Into a Savings Opportunity

Depending on your income, you may be eligible for government subsidies.

These need to be sent to the concerned government agencies along with the corresponding declaration of your previous year's income.

There are also additional qualifications depending on what subsidy you are applying for, whether it's for daycare subsidy, rent subsidy or tuition subsidy.

In our case, we qualified for a 50% subsidy for our monthly rent in our first year in Canada.

Back then that was around $400 in savings each month.

However, it is important that you declare any changes in income and in status to avoid having to pay this money back.

We also qualified to receive daycare subsidies for our two children.

Mind you, daycare is not cheap.
It can sometimes cost as much as your monthly salary, depending on the age of your child and how many children you are sending to daycare.

In our case, my husband and I decided to put both kids in daycare so that the two of us could work at the same time.

Through this, we were able to figure out how we ultimately wanted to live our lives in Canada.

We calculated that even with both kids in daycare, we would still be able to save money with both of us working instead of just one.

Another way is through your local food bank.
This is an actual photo of the first stash we received from our local food bank.
It was actually more than enough to supplement our meals.

You just have to be creative and look at the different ingredients that you can use in order to make this into a complete meal.

I still remember the first time I went to the local food bank. There was already a line of people waiting outside the building, each bringing his own bag or his own trolley.

I saw someone who looked unclean and who did not speak good English.

It dawned on me that these people needed the food bank more than I did.

While I may not have a job, I can still afford to buy us groceries. But those people? The food bank might be all they have to be able to eat.

I felt guilty for being there!

But the good thing is that there was no judgment from anyone there.

As long as you're there, you have the same rights as everyone else to receive the same food.

I just got what was good enough for our family and made sure to not get anything that we wouldn't otherwise eat.

I stopped going to the local food bank when I got a job. I was happy to leave it to the people who needed it the most.

What's the big message here?
My big message is to be humble and learn to accept support.

When we decided to land in British Columbia, we knew we had no family or friends in BC.

During our last few days in the Philippines, we learned that my husband has a distant relative living in Vancouver.

When we arrived, she picked us up from the airport.

That's when we first met. She took us out to dinner after a long flight from the Philippines.

Occasionally, she would visit us at home, bring us groceries.

Now, six years later, she still fills our freezer with food!

For that, we are very grateful for the money we were able to save.

What Would You Rather Have?
A car or $400 per month?

There's no right or wrong decision here.
Only a smart one.

We are now a family of six, and yet, we do not own a car in Canada.

Never rented one, never drove one.

We've been lucky in that our neighborhood has a high walk score. Meaning, all essential services are within walking distance of our home.

Would you like to go to the groceries? A 10-minute walk?

Do you need to go to the hospital? It's only a three minute walk across the street.

Church every week? A 10-minute walk.

The kids' school is another 10 minute walk.

If we want to travel far enough that we need a bus ride, the bus stop is just a seven minute walk from our house.

The secret is to plan in advance when you need to leave in order to catch the hourly bus. The bus ride itself has been an adventure for the entire family.

Occasionally we would take a cab.

I know cabs can be expensive.

But even with cabs every weekend, it still wouldn't amount to the cost of gasoline and insurance we would otherwise pay if we owned a car.

In some provinces and in some suburbs, public transportation is not as widely available.

In winter, it becomes especially hard to wait for a bus under the freezing cold, or even walk to places with knee-high snow.

If that's the case, a car might be a wise investment.

Take note, owning a car also opens you up to higher paying jobs.

It might also allow you to take on a side job like food delivery.

So think about it and weigh the pros and cons of owning a car versus just taking public transportation.

Heard of the Immigrant Saving Money But Wearing Branded Clothes and Eating Out?

It could be you!

You don't have to deprive yourself of eating out and good quality branded clothes just because you're trying to save money.

Almost all major fast food companies offer discount coupons.

The secret is to just Google "restaurant name" + coupon + the name of your province, and download it to your phone.

Kaching! Money saved!

As for thrift stores, listen to me first.

I know that it can get icky wearing pre-loved clothes.
I know because I didn't buy into that idea right away either.

But give it a chance, and you will discover that most clothes are still in good condition. Most clothes are clean, some still have their original tags on them and have never been used before.

Some of the best buys you can find in thrift stores are winter jackets.

Winter jackets can easily cost you at least $100 for a brand new, high-quality pair of jackets. But at thrift stores, you can get them for $40!

The other thing is baby clothes. We all know babies grow fast.

I have two kids born in Canada and the clothes I bought from thrift stores were still in very good condition, almost brand new. The colors were still very bright.

In fact, they're still very much in good condition that I was able to pass it on to another child.

Cookware is also a good find in thrift stores.
You know, the traditional, branded cookware? The heavy ones?
I bought mine from thrift stores when we first arrived in Canada.

Six years later, I still use them. No chips, no cracks, no stains.
And to think that I cook every day, eh?

What else is worth your money at thrift shops?
Hmmmm, let's see.

Practically everything! I'll let you discover it for yourself!

To Immigrants Who Want To Start Saving Money But Can't Get Started

Now that you have extra money each month, where should that money go?

How do you make sure that this money goes to savings, not just to other expenses?

Where should you invest?

Now is a good time to start building an actual savings fund.

The first step is to set up an auto transfer from your payroll account to your savings account.

This way you are paying yourself first and setting aside a certain amount of money for your savings. You are then forced to live on whatever is left.

Take note, however, that savings will not grow as much if you just leave it with the bank.

And this is where government programs come in!

In the next few pages, I will share with you two of the investment programs that are currently offered by the government. These are the easiest to start with when you're just starting out in Canada.

The first is the **RESP or the Registered Education Savings Program.**
This is a special savings account for parents who want to save for their child's
education after high school.

This is where money received from the Canada Education Savings Grant is
deposited, which is equivalent to 20% of your contributions.

In short, CESG gives you a 20% return on whatever you're contributing up to
a maximum of $500 each year.

Where else can you get a 20% interest on your money nowadays?

Another investment opportunity is the **TFSA or the Tax Free Savings
Account.** This is for adults 18 years and older.

This is a way for individuals who have a valid social insurance number to set
aside money tax free throughout their lifetime.

Any amount contributed, as well as any income earned in this account, is
generally tax free, even if withdrawn.

There are other investment and savings programs that you can invest in as
your income grows. Be sure to talk to your registered financial advisor so that
he or she can walk you through your options.

If you don't know anyone, feel free to send me a message at
familimigrant@gmail.com.

I'd be happy to refer you to my trusted financial advisor.

Discover The Fortune That Lies Hidden In Your Expenses

In Canada, you have to file and submit your tax return by April of next year. This means preparing your own tax returns.

I know it can be inconvenient and difficult in the beginning, but this is where fortune lies.

You can deduct your prescribed medicines, charitable donations, church tithes, daycare fees, and even tuition fees that you've paid for yourself, based on your gross income.

Disclaimer: I am not a tax expert.

I am only sharing what I have experienced in my years of preparing tax returns for myself and my family in British Columbia.

There are differences among provinces. There will be differences in marital status, qualified dependents, and even income status. So your tax situation is unique to my tax situation.

If you're not sure, research and consult an accountant.

There is also free tax software that you can download and use to prepare tax returns for yourself.

These are the most popular ones in Canada. I personally use SimpleTax.

As of this writing, SimpleTax is now Wealthsimple

In our first year, my husband and I received a refund from the tax revenue agency because we had a lot of deductible expenses in our first year.

We had almost all the deductions we could qualify for: tuition fees, daycare fees, prescribed medications and charitable donations.

So it was nice to have received a refund.

Now, what should you do with your tax refund?

No, you won't be buying a new guitar with your tax refund.

Don't make it a habit to treat your tax refund as a bonus you have received.

It is not money that you can use to buy something you otherwise wouldn't buy if you didn't have the money.

The truth is, it's not actually a bonus!

It's actually money you've already paid to the government and gotten back with no interest!

Still, it's better than not getting it back.

This is why you should invest in higher return investments to regain that lost opportunity.

You can invest this money back in an RESP or TFSA. Speak to your registered financial advisor as to where best to put that money.

Epilogue

That wraps up our Best Kept Canadian Immigrant Secrets!

My wish is for you to be able to successfully apply these learnings to your everyday life in Canada so that you will be a successful Canadian immigrant.

Thank you for being here and for taking this journey with me.

Whether you've already landed in Canada, are still waiting for your visa or are just in the process of researching whether Canadian immigration is for you:

Congratulations on taking the first step towards your Canadian dream!

Not many people take the first step towards their dreams.
It sets you apart!

In fact, you even took it a step further by deciding that you could succeed as a Canadian immigrant by purchasing this book.

So pat yourself on the back and give yourself a high five.

Tell yourself, "Congratulations! You did it, you're successful."

To learn more, please visit: https://www.facebook.com/familimigrant.
You can send me a message through that page.

Ask me questions, share your comments, and tell me stories!

I would love to hear them.

Also, don't forget to claim your exclusive membership to the Canadian Immigrant Secrets - Inner Circle. Only for owners of this book!

You can ask more questions there, and get more support from people who have also been in the same situation as you.

That's a community of new immigrants, of those who are still deciding, and those who are still waiting for their visas to arrive.

Thank you again for taking this journey with me.

Good luck!

I wish you all the best in your new life in Canada.

FamiliMigrant Programs To Help You in Your Canadian Journey

Do you want more help? Choose any of the programs below:

1. Experience this book in video form. Get the e-course here: https://andreavchiu.com/familimigrant-canadian-immigrant-best-kept-secrets/

2. Get your exclusive membership to the Canadian Immigrant Inner circle! Only for those who purchased this book. Join here: https://www.facebook.com/groups/canadianimmigrantsecretsinnercircle

3. Canada newcomers, do you want to be stable and be comfortable in your new life in Canada within 90 days? Join the 90-Day 1-on-1 Mentoring where you will get personal and customized guidance on the things you need to do to be successful in Canada. Send an email to familimigrant@gmail.com to apply.

4. Follow Andrea and her family's Canada adventures (and misadventures) in https://www.facebook.com/familimigrant

Acknowledgement

If you know me, it would come as a big surprise to you that I have written a book.

What is perhaps even more surprising is that I'm sharing my stories openly to readers I haven't even met.

This is definitely way outside my own private personality.

This wouldn't have been possible without my mentor, *Jomar Hilario*, who generously shares his time and knowledge. For teaching me ways to share my stories with the world, for opening my eyes to opportunities, for shifting my mindset.

To my *No Face family*, who've been my constant companions throughout the year this book and my ecourse was published.

For the support, critiques, reviews and shares, for showing up at our weekly meetings and sharing your thoughts on the topic.

For believing in me, appreciating my work and motivating me. In you, I've found new friends. In you, I've gained wisdom.

Troy, thank you for always supporting me in everything I do.

No questions asked.

For always listening to my endless stories and brainstorms, for always believing in me.

Theo, thank you for being my fan and for finding me "cool" in what I do.

Cielo, thank you for being such a responsible big sister. Always looking after the younger kids when I'm in a meeting or working on something.

Thank you *Ellie* for being so understanding of my work at such a young age.

Thank you *Paolo* for being who you are, forcing Mommy to take a break, rest and spend time with you.

Thank you to our families in the Philippines for supporting us in our new lives in Canada.

To all who have helped us on our Canadian journey, a huge thank you.

About the Author

Andrea was originally from the Philippines. She moved to BC, Canada in 2015.

That same year, she started the Filipino Immigrant in Canada Facebook page to document her experiences as a Canadian immigrant. As the page gained followers, it started receiving questions from aspiring immigrants to Canada.

In 2020, after almost six years of living in Canada, she started FamiliMigrant to share her experiences and the lessons she's learned as a Canadian immigrant.

Her goal was to help new and aspiring Canadian immigrants adjust and succeed in their new lives.

Thus, the publication of this book, along with the e-course Best Kept Canadian Immigrant Secrets.

She's a mom of four kids who keeps her busy all day.

When she's not thinking of something new to do, or learning a new skill, she's out with her husband thrift-shopping and trying out new restaurants in their small town.

She loves going on simple dates and exploring her city by foot or by bus.